Caring for Creation
Reflections on the Biblical Basis of Earthcare

Lisa Lofland Gould

Friends Committee on Unity With Nature

© Copyright 1999
Friends Committee on Unity with Nataure

Friends Committee on Unity With Nature
173-B N. Prospect St.
Burlington, VT 05401-1607
802/658-0308
fcun@together.net

10 9 8 7 6 5 4 3 2 1
ISBN: 1-881083-05-5
Library of Congress number: 99-72762

Publication of this book was made possible
in part by a generous donation from
the Obadiah Brown Benevolent Fund.

Cover art:
"Noah's Ark" by Edward Hicks
by permission of Philadelphia Museum of Art
bequest of Lisa Norris Elkins

See page 96 for other permissions and credits

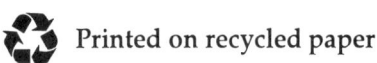 Printed on recycled paper

Caring for Creation
*Reflections on the
Biblical Basis of Earthcare*

Contents

Introduction 1

1. Celebration 7

2. Humus 23

3. Connections 37

4. Right Relationship 53

5. Stewardship 69

Using *Caring For Creation* in Your Meeting........... 85

Literature Cited 94

*You visit the earth and water it, you greatly enrich it.
The river of God is full of water....*

Psalm 65:9

Introduction

This book arose from the "Bible Half-Hour" talks given at the 336th session of New England Yearly Meeting, held in August 1996. The theme of the sessions that year was adapted from Micah 6:8: *What does the Lord require of me?*

When asked to do these talks, I was requested to share what has come from me and through me—in my life as a natural being, biologist, and Friend—and to tell of how the Bible spoke to me about caring for Creation. Sheer terror was my initial reaction, for it will be obvious to the reader that I am not a Bible scholar and lay no claim to such.

Much of my background has been in the academic arena. My father was a professor, my husband is a professor, and I have taught and lectured for many years in a university setting. So my first impulse, once I agreed to give the talks, was to hide myself in a library for a year and become a scholar on the Bible and Creation. (Actually, that was my second impulse; my first was to move to Tibet so I wouldn't have to deal with it!) But the more I thought about and prayed over the talks, the more I realized that I had to resist the urge to do what would have been, for me, the easy route: the academic approach.

And so I tried a different way. I read the Bible straight through that year, trying to read it again with fresh eyes, the eyes of the heart. I strove to be open to what was given me. Each time I was tempted to run out and read what *real* Bible scholars have to say on the subject (and there is much fine work in print), I gave myself a mental rap and tried instead to center down and seek the Light through worship and the words of the Bible.

Several major themes arose as I read. First was the need to *celebrate*—the Bible is full of so many references to the glory and beauty of Creation and to the joy we can derive from it! But *humility* followed swiftly, in my awareness of how vast Creation is and how little we human beings really understand of it, at any level, scientific or spiritual.

The Bible is also a primer on understanding our place in our communities and our *connections* with our fellow human beings and the rest of Creation. I became aware of how many gifts we have to help us connect—our senses, our intellect, our imagination—and how we can use these gifts to help bring us back into *right relationship* with Creation. For there is no question in my mind that the vast majority of human society is no longer in harmony with Creation. The *physical* evidence of the harm we are doing is obvious; the Bible, and Friends such as John Woolman, help us see the *spiritual* damage we are doing.

And so I came finally to *stewardship,* to exploring how we got into this predicament, and how we might learn to live as Jesus taught us—and as our Quaker faith and practice so clearly inform us—to truly love our neighbors—*all* our neighbors—as ourselves.

Introduction

At the sessions themselves, each day's talk was given out of the silence of worship, and worship continued afterwards. What follows here is basically the text of the talks as they were given to New England Yearly Meeting. It has been modified mainly to make it more understandable to a reading audience and to smooth out a few rough spots.

Lisa Lofland Gould

Acknowledgments

I am extremely grateful to the support that was given to me during the months of preparation and at the 1996 sessions of New England Yearly Meeting at Bowdoin College, Brunswick, Maine. In particular I would like to thank the planners of the 1996 NEYM sessions, for giving me the challenge; the members of the New England Friends in Unity With Nature Committee (NEFUN), for all their help; and the members of Friends Committee on Unity with Nature (FCUN), from whom I never stop learning. Thanks go also to Jan Hoffman, who always knew when and how to give just the support that was needed; to Bob Hillegass, for his kind introduction; to my husband, Mark, who was an irreplaceable prop during the days leading up to and during the talks; and to all the Friends who responded so thoughtfully and warmly to the talks.

Thanks also go to Barbara Bennett Mays, editor of Friends United Press, for her thoughtful comments as this manuscript neared completion.

Finally, much gratitude goes to Ruah Swennerfelt and Louis Cox for their careful oversight in the final stages of publication.

*Praise the Lord from the earth,
you sea monsters and all deeps....*
Psalm 148:7

1. Celebration

Make a joyful noise unto the Lord, all ye lands.
Psalm 66:1

1. *Praise the Lord! Praise the Lord from the heavens; praise him from the heights!*
2. *Praise him, all his angels! praise him all his host!*
3. *Praise him, sun and moon;*
4. *Praise him, you highest heavens, and you waters above the heavens!*
5. *Let them praise the name of the Lord, for he commanded and they were created.*
6. *He established them forever and ever; he fixed their bounds, which cannot be passed.*
7. *Praise the Lord from the earth, you sea monsters and all deeps,*
8. *fire and hail, snow and frost, stormy wind fulfilling his command.*
9. *Mountains and all hills, fruit trees and all cedars!*
10. *Wild animals and all cattle, creeping things and flying birds!*
11. *Kings of the earth and all peoples, princes and all rulers of the earth!*
12. *Young men and women alike, old and young together!*

¹³ *Let them praise the name of the Lord, for his name alone is exalted; his glory is above earth and heaven.*

Psalm 148:1–13

⁶ *Let everything that breathes praise the Lord! Praise the Lord!*

Psalm 150:6

These lines from Psalms 148 and 150 express the writer's appreciation for God's creation, and how all of Creation stretches to be in contact with the Divine Creator. I love the part about the sea monsters—can't you just see all the sea monsters coming to the surface of the sea and shouting "Yay, Lord!"?

The Bible is a primer on celebrating Creation, and of trying to understand our place in it. The Bible reminds us over and over of the splendor of Creation, of how little human beings understand it, and of how to be in right relationship to it, to one another, to and the Creator. And there's no question that the Creator was pleased with this work: *God saw everything that he had made, and indeed, it was very good* [Genesis 1:31]. How could we be so ungrateful as to *not* enjoy and celebrate Creation?

For centuries people have puzzled over the human place in Creation, wondering how we fit into the pattern that we call life on Earth. What *are* our connections with each other, and our connections with the other beings with which we share this planet? What does the Bible—and other revelations—have to say about those connections and relationships, and how they can help guide us?

The Bible is first and foremost the story of a group of people and their relationship with the Creator, but it is also is full of wonderful images from the non-human world. What do the great prophets do when they want to be closest to God? They go into the wilderness, where there are no people to corrupt the relationship between them and the Divine Spirit. Moses, John the Baptist, and Jesus are all mentioned as seeking the wilderness, the purity of God's creation. When important things happen, it is often on mountaintops: the landing of the Ark on Mount Ararat, the giving of the Ten Commandments on Mount Sinai, the Sermon on the Mount, Jesus praying in the Garden of Gethsemane on the Mount of Olives.

Wind and water obey God's command: the Flood rises that only Noah and the Ark escape; the Red Sea parts for Moses, and the River Jordan for Elijah and Elisha; and Elijah is taken to heaven in a whirlwind. Jesus calms the waters of the Sea of Galilee and the water holds him up. And the whole earth darkens and quakes when Jesus dies on the cross.

And animals and plants do amazing things in the Bible: the Serpent tempts Adam and Eve, a dove brings the olive branch to Noah, Balaam's donkey can see the angel even when Balaam can't, the ravens feed Elijah, the lions refuse to feed on Daniel, and a great fish eats Jonah and then spews him out again. A grumpy Elisha summons bears to come out and maul some boys who are taunting him. Locusts, poisonous snakes, and plagues of mice punish the disobedient; and the Gadarene swine carry off evil spirits. God's voice is heard through a burning bush, and mushrooms feed the people during their forty years in the wilderness (many scholars believe that "manna" was a fungus). While Jonah is off pouting because God has decided not to destroy Nineveh, God has a shrub grow up to shade him from the sun. And in a beautiful plant image, Jesus is spoken of as the "true vine" and God as the vinegrower; the followers of Jesus are the branches and fruit.

I especially love the water images in the Bible—what could have been a more stirring image to desert people? In Revelation and elsewhere God's voice is "the sound of many waters." And water images often describe how people long to be in right relationship with the Creator, as here in the Psalms:

> 1 *As a deer longs for flowing streams, so my soul longs for you, O God....*
> 7 *Deep calls to deep at the thunders of your cataracts, all your waves and your billows have gone over me....*
>
> Psalm 42:1, 7

> 9 *You visit the earth and water it, you greatly enrich it, The river of God is full of water...*
> 12 *The pastures of the wilderness overflow, the hills gird themselves with joy,*
> 13 *the meadows clothe themselves with flocks, the valleys deck themselves with grain, they shout and sing together for joy.*
>
> Psalm 65:9; 12–13

> 7 *Singers and dancers alike say, "All my springs are in you."*
>
> Psalm 87:7

What Friends do not resonate to this from Amos:

> *But let justice roll down like waters, and righteousness like an everflowing stream.*
>
> Amos 5:24

The New Testament speaks of "living water," with the story of Jesus and the Samaritan woman at the well; Jesus tells the people in John 7:37–39, "*Let anyone who is thirsty come to me, and let the one who believes in me drink. As the scripture has said, 'Out of the believer's heart shall flow rivers of living water'.*"

The Bible also offers many images of what will happen when the human and non-human world live together in harmony and obedience to the laws of the Creator:

> *6 The wolf shall live with the lamb, the leopard shall lie down with the kid, the calf and the lion and the fatling together, and a little child shall lead them.*
> *7 The cow and the bear shall graze, their young shall lie down together and the lion shall eat straw like the ox.*
> *8 The nursing child shall play over the hole of the asp, and the weaned child shall put its hand into the adder's den.*
> *9 They will not hurt or destroy on all my holy mountain; for the earth will be full of the knowledge of the Lord, as the waters cover the sea.*
>
> Isaiah 11:6–9

When the people repent and return to a covenant relationship, Isaiah tells us that all Creation will rejoice:

> *12 For you shall go out in joy, and be led back in peace; the mountains and the hills before you shall burst into song, and all the trees of the field shall clap their hands.*
> *13 Instead of the thorn shall come up the cypress; instead of the brier shall come up the myrtle; and it shall be to the Lord for a memorial, for an everlasting sign that shall not be cut off.*
>
> Isaiah 55:12–13

These images of joyous mountaintops and amazing animals, of wondrous weather and obliging plants, fire the imagination and inspire us to this day, many thousands of years after the stories were written. But there is still wonder and inspiration, all around us, here and now. I know an amazing organism. It begins to grow in the middle of winter, sometimes coming into bloom in January or February. It has such a high metabolic rate that it can melt through snow, and maintains a temperature of 72 degrees Fahrenheit, even in the chill of winter. Because it's so warm, it provides shelter for a great variety of creatures: one scientist counted 26 different species of insects, sowbugs, spiders and other invertebrates resting, mating, and living within the flower of this plant in the winter. The plant is pollinated by winter-active flies that are attracted to the special odor of this plant, an odor that people have noticed too, and have given it the name "Skunk Cabbage." Take a close-up look at a Skunk Cabbage flower next time you walk in wet winter woods.

Another amazing creation comes to my mind: There's a tree that blooms late in the year, its golden flowers opening as the leaves are also changing to gold. If you pay attention to this tree earlier in the summer, you'll notice that several insects use this plant. One kind of moth likes to lay its eggs on the leaves and rolls them up nicely from the tip of the leaf down toward the base. Another moth rolls its eggs from the side of the leaf. You might also find a little red gall that forms on the leaves, looking like a tiny witch's hat, or like a "Hershey's Kiss" candy, some say. Inside the gall is the larva of an aphid; when it leaves the gall, it will feed on the host plant where the mother aphid laid the egg. The aphid's name is *Hormaphis hamamelidis,* which means, basically, an aphid which associates with the Witch Hazel tree. Here, similar to the Skunk Cabbage, is a whole community of organisms living together.

Or what about this wondrous plant? It has hundreds of tiny flowers that radiate out from its center, the florets on the outer edges of the flower head opening earliest. Bees and other insects love to visit the flowers for their nectar and pollen; the whole flower head closes up at night or in the rain, to protect that precious nectar and pollen from dew and falling rain. Take a close look and you can see the curling tips of the female stigmas and the blunt pollen-covered male stamens. After pollination, the stem of this plant elongates, for the seeds have tiny parachutes, and only by reaching up into the breezes above the grasses will they be launched on their way. I'm talking, of course, about the Common Dandelion.

We don't need to visit tropical rainforests or exotic locales to see these wonders; we don't have to make a trip to the Grand Canyon or Yosemite—or watch the Discovery Channel—to be awed by the mystery and integrity of Creation. It is all around us, in our house plants, our yards, the compost heap, the dust under the sofa, the neighborhood park—*Everywhere* is great beauty, complexity, amazement. "Love of nature" is in so many ways a silly term; for some people it means love of scenic beauty—which is only a tiny part of the real grandness of "nature" (and in any case dichotomizing, as if there were something that *wasn't* nature, which of course there isn't)—everything, from the rocks to the spirit, are part of Creation.

The Earth is the Lord's and the fullness thereof.

Psalm 24:1

Who among us is not nurtured by a look at the stars on a clear night... the touch of snowflakes against our upturned face... a glimpse of the first crocus poking through the snow... the sound of water rushing over pebbles on the beach... the liquid call of a thrush... the sight of moonlight on water... the feel of a velvety patch of moss... the first hint of fall color... the scent of rain in the spring...the sky's glow at sunset... the spring peepers calling on March night... the brilliance of a rainbow after a July thunderstorm—Think of these, and how much they mean to us! This is not sentimentality; these are essential to our being, for they uphold us and remind us that we are not alone, that we are part of something very great.

Nor do we need to be outside to appreciate and enjoy "nature"—it's right here, around us and within us. Our own bodies are a source of wonder: Listen to words from Psalm 139: *"I praise you, for I am fearfully and wonderfully made. Wonderful are your works; that I know very well."* And think of the amazing things our bodies can do! We can dance and sing; we can walk and hop and skip; we can swim and weave and build and hoe and make love and write and knit and play golf. We have been given the gift of a wide range of senses, many channels in which to "tune in" the messages of Creation. It is important to remind ourselves, however, that human senses are not the full range possible—there are things we cannot hear, we cannot see, we cannot touch or smell, that other beings are attuned to.

Celebration

God is aware that the senses are important to people. Look at the instructions given the Israelites involving the Ark of the Covenant and the creation of the tabernacle. At least six or seven chapters of Exodus are given over to describing how to build the Ark of the Covenant, the table at the altar, the tabernacle itself, the tent over the tabernacle, the sacred court, the altar for sacrifices, and the priestly vestments, with very precise instructions about using the most precious fibers, ores, stones, spices, and woods to create a home fit for holding the Ark and worshipping God. For years these chapters bothered me—I couldn't figure out why God wanted all these fancy trappings, when just a few chapters before, God had told people to make altars of earth and unhewn stone, unpolluted by human hands. God seemed to be Quaker one minute, and Catholic the next! But then it came to me that these people, wandering in a desert of stones and earth, may have needed something very different, something which appealed to all their senses in a unique way. Joseph Campbell wrote that one of the objects in worship is to be "thrown out" of your usual state of mind. Surely this amazing collection of scents and sounds and sights and textures must have put the Israelites in a different frame of mind.

Our relationships with other people are also part of the grandeur and wonder of Creation. What a beautiful expression of young love is in these lines from the Song of Solomon:

> [8] *The voice of my beloved! Look, he comes leaping upon the mountains, bounding over the hills.*
> [9] *My beloved is like a gazelle or a young stag. Look, there he*

> *stands behind our wall, gazing in at the windows, looking through the lattice.*
> ¹⁰ *My beloved speaks and says to me: "Arise, my love, my fair one, and come away;*
> ¹¹ *for now the winter is past, the rain is over and gone.*
> ¹² *The flowers appear on the earth; the time of singing has come, and the voice of the turtledove is heard in our land.*
> ¹³ *The fig tree puts forth its figs, and the vines are in blossom; they give forth fragrance. Arise, my love, my fair one, and come away.*
> ¹⁴ *O my dove, in the clefts of the rock, in the covert of the cliff, let me see your face, let me hear your voice; for your voice is sweet, and you face is lovely."*
> Song of Solomon 2:8–14

Our human relationships—the giving and receiving of love—are truly to be celebrated as part of the divine Creation. The whole of the New Testament is taken up with our relationship with the Spirit and with each other:

Jesus says,*"This is my commandment, that you love one another as I have loved you"* [John 15:12].

For human beings, of course, our love for each other and for the rest of Creation is tinged with great poignancy, in the knowledge that we will die, that our senses may fade and our steps become more halting. This awareness should not lessen our joy in Creation, but make us more eager than ever to celebrate our place in the pattern of life, of which death and decay are as much a part as birth and growth. Hear the words of Ecclesiastes:

> ¹ *For everything there is a season, and a time for every matter under heaven:*

Celebration

> [2] *a time to be born, and a time to die; a time to plant, and a time to pluck up that which is planted;*
> [3] *a time to kill, and a time to heal; a time to break down, and a time to build up;*
> [4] *a time to weep, and a time to laugh; a time to mourn, and a time to dance;*
> [5] *a time to cast away stones, and a time to gather stones together; a time to embrace, and a time to refrain from embracing;*
> [6] *a time to seek, and a time to lose; a time to keep, and a time to throw away;*
> [7] *a time to tear, and a time to sew; a time to keep silence, and a time to speak;*
> [8] *a time to love, and a time to hate; a time for war, and a time for peace.*
>
> Ecclesiastes 3:1–8

For myself, I am increasingly aware of how easily I slip from the pattern of constant celebration and appreciation of living. Over the past several years I've talked with many people about the issue of right relationship with *time*. How easily I, for one—and apparently many others, from what I glean from my friends and the media—become embroiled in the daily "busyness" of my work life and other obvious duties, and ignore the need for recreation, for time away from desk and papers and telephones and "should-do's." The great collective lament of modern life—and I suspect part of what has led to our apathy and our sense of exhaustion—is this perceived burden of Not Enough Time. In this light, in recent months I have been thinking more about the concept of the Sabbath and just what it means, especially in this area of our relationship with time. As you know, one of the

Ten Commandments God gave to the Israelites was about keeping the Sabbath:

> [8] *Remember the sabbath day, and keep it holy.*
> [9] *Six days shall you labor and do all your work.*
> [10] *But on the seventh day is a sabbath to the Lord your God; you shall not do any work—you, your son or your daughter, your male or female slave, your livestock, or the alien resident in your towns.*
> [11] *For in six days the Lord made heaven and earth, the sea, and all that is in them, but rested the seventh day; therefore the Lord blessed the sabbath day and consecrated it.*
>
> Exodus 20:8–11

The sabbath laws in the Old Testament are very rigid and detailed, going so far as to recommend death for those not keeping the laws. In the New Testament, however, Jesus scandalized the priests by allowing the disciples to pluck grain to eat on the Sabbath and by healing on the Sabbath. In Mark 2:27, Jesus made clear his understanding of the Sabbath: *"The sabbath was made for humankind, and not humankind for the sabbath."* The Sabbath is a way to increase our joy in life, giving us space to maintain a proper relationship with the Creator.

Isaiah tells us:

> [1] *Thus says the Lord: Maintain justice, and do what is right, for soon my salvation will come and my deliverance be revealed.*
> [2] *Happy is the mortal who does this, the one who holds it fast, who keeps the sabbath, not profaning it, and refrains from doing any evil.*
>
> Isaiah 56:1–2

And Ecclesiastes reminds us that the key word here is *happiness:*

> ¹⁵ *So I command enjoyment, for there is nothing better for people under the sun than to eat, and drink, and enjoy themselves, for this will go with them in their toil through the days of life that God gives them under the sun.*
>
> Ecclesiastes 8:15

How do we "keep the Sabbath" in these modern times? For Friends, of course, worship can be held on any day and at any time; "Sunday" is just First Day, and the other religious holidays were traditionally ignored by early Friends. But when Friends were forming, the surrounding society kept many of the Sabbath customs, which probably meant that Friends, too, refrained from "business as usual" on First Days. Now our secular society has gone far, far away from the old Sabbath laws: On First Days stores are open, ans business meetings are held: we travel long distances, and mostly do virtually anything we do on a weekday. Few of us would go back to the old days of following the letter of the Sabbath laws, but how do we nourish the spirit of the Sabbath on all days? How do we seek to "come 'round right" in our relationship with time, a key part of "coming 'round right" in our relationship with the pattern of Creation, and one of the deep changes we must make in order to weave ourselves back into a wholesome part of the pattern?

To start, let us seek to be always open to the wonder, mystery, and integrity of Creation. We are called to enjoy life! We are called to celebrate!

[1] *Make a joyful noise to the Lord, all the earth.*
[2] *Worship the Lord with gladness; come into his presence with singing.*
[3] *Know that the Lord is God. It is he that made us, and we are his; we are his people, and the sheep of his pasture.*
[4] *Enter his gates with thanksgiving, and his courts with praise. Give thanks to him, bless his name.*
[5] *For the Lord is good; his steadfast love endures forever, and his faithfulness to all generations.*

Psalm 100:1–5

Go to the ant, you lazybones; consider its ways, and be wise.

Proverbs 6:6

2. Humus

*Where were you when I laid
the foundations of the earth?*
                    Job 38:4

[12] But where shall wisdom be found? And where is the place of understanding?
[13] Mortals do not know the way to it, and it is not found in the land of the living.
[14] The deep says, "It is not in me," and the sea says, "It is not with me."
[15] It cannot be gotten for gold, and silver cannot be weighed out as its price.
[20] Where then does wisdom come from? And where is the place of understanding?
[21] It is hidden from the eyes of all living, and concealed from the birds of the air....
[22] God understands the way to it, and he knows its place.
[24] For he looks to the ends of the earth, and sees everything under the heavens.
[25] When he gave the wind its weight, and apportioned out the waters by measure;
[26] when he made a decree for the rain, and a way for the thunderbolt;

²⁷ *then he saw it and declared it; he established it and searched it out.*
²⁸ *And he said to humankind, "Truly, the fear of the Lord, that is Wisdom; and to depart from evil is understanding."*
                                                                    Job 28:12–28

What does it mean to fear the Lord, and what does this have to do with caring for the Earth? The word "fear" in relationship to God used to bother me a great deal. If I were to be in a loving relationship with the Creator, which is certainly what I hoped for, and what the New Testament promises, *fear* seemed to me to be out of place, a disharmony. So I went to the Oxford English Dictionary and discovered over four columns on the word *fear*, which has as one of its meanings, "to be in awe of, to revere." It appears that the word probably ultimately comes from an Aramaic root meaning "to go through, to pass through." Might "fear of the Lord" be the process of going from our ordinary, daily doings into a state of recognition that there is something greater than we are? That we are only a part of something much grander than we can ever, with our limited human abilities, imagine?

These are things that many of our Quaker "saints" have written about. William Penn reminds us to seek an understanding of our place in Creation:

> *It would go a great way to caution and direct people in their Use of the World, that they were better studied and known in the Creation of it. For How can Man find the confidence to abuse it, while they should see the Great Creator stare them in the face, in all and every Part thereof?*

George Fox tells us that Christ is "that Wisdom which is pure from above, which is gentle and easy to be entreated, not hurtful, nor destructive, but is to the preserving of the whole creation."

And John Woolman notes: "I saw that an humble man, with the blessing of the Lord, might live on a little, and that where the heart was set on greatness, success in business did not satisfy the craving; but that commonly with an increase of wealth the desire of wealth increased. There was a care on my mind so to pass my time that nothing might hinder me from the most steady attention to the voice of the true Shepherd."

Are we humble in the face of Creation? Or do we think we have all the answers, or if not all the answers, can fix up our mistakes with our technological prowess? Do we give lip service to humility, but secretly resonate with Mordred's line from his song "The 7 Deadly Virtues" in the musical *Camelot:* "I find humility means to be hurt, it's not the earth the meek inherit, it's the dirt"?

Mystics of all traditions are aware of the importance of a sense of humility, of accepting ourselves as part of the Earth. The word *humble* comes from the same Latin root as *humus,* meaning the ground or soil; the word for man, *homo,* also has the same root. And the same is true for the Hebrew words "Adam," which means *man,* and "adamah," which means *soil.* If you are a gardener, you already have a sense of the beauty of soil, the feel of it between your fingers, the smell of the good spring earth. It helps to remember that the soil is that from which things grow. To be humble, to be soil, is to participate in the regeneration of the Earth.

Certainly the Bible reminds us, over and over, of how little we know! Listen to the words of God in response to Job's queries:

4 *Where were you when I laid the foundation of the earth? Tell me, if you have understanding.*
5 *Who determined its measurements—surely you know!*
6 *On what were its bases sunk, or who laid its cornerstone*
7 *when the morning stars sang together and all the heavenly beings shouted for joy?*
8 *Or who shut in the sea with doors when it burst out from the womb?—*
9 *when I made the clouds its garment, and thick darkness its swaddling band,*
10 *and prescribed bounds for it, and set bars and doors*
11 *and said, "Thus far shall you come, and no farther, and here shall your proud waves be stopped."?*
12 *Have you commanded the morning since your days began, and caused the dawn to know its place,*
13 *so that it might take hold of the skirts of the earth, and the wicked be shaken out of it?*

16 *Have you entered into the springs of the sea, or walked in the recesses of the deep?*
17 *Have the gates of death been revealed to you, or have you seen the gates of deep darkness?*
18 *Have you comprehended the expanse of the earth? Declare, if you know all this.*
19 *Where is the way to the dwelling of light, and where is the place of darkness,*
20 *that you may take it to its territory and that you may discern the paths to its home?*
21 *Surely you know, for you were born then, and the number of your days is great!*

^{22} *Have you entered the storehouses of the snow, or have you seen the storehouses of the hail,*
^{23} *which I have reserved for the time of trouble, for the day of battle and war?*
^{24} *What is the way to the place where the light is distributed, or where the east wind is scattered upon the earth?*
^{25} *Who has cut a channel for the torrents of rain, and a way for the thunderbolt,*
^{26} *to bring rain on a land where no one lives, on the desert, which is empty of human life,*
^{27} *to satisfy the waste and desolate land, and to make the ground put forth grass?*

Job 38:4–13; 16–27

God makes it clear here that God's actions aren't just to please people—it rains even where there are no people, if you can imagine that!

Isaiah also admonishes us to keep straight the relationship of who has true knowledge and understanding:

^{16} *You turn things upside down! Shall the potter be regarded as the clay? Shall the thing made say of its maker, "He did not make me"; or the thing formed say of the one who formed it, "He has no understanding"?*

Isaiah 29:16

And lest we ever slip up and forget, the Bible constantly reminds us human beings what a troublesome lot we are, and that God cares for the whole of Creation, not just people. After the Flood, Noah and his family build an altar and offer burnt sacrifices:

^{21} *And when the Lord smelled the pleasing odor, the Lord said in his heart, "I will never again curse the ground*

because of humankind, for the inclination of the human heart is evil from youth; nor will I every again destroy every living creature as I have done.
²² As long as the earth endures, seedtime and harvest, cold and heat, summer and winter, day and night shall not cease."

Genesis 8:21–22

Job notes:

⁶ For misery does not come from the earth, nor does trouble sprout from the ground,
⁷ but human beings are born to trouble just as sparks fly upward.

Job 5:6–7

And we are told, depressingly, how our works can corrupt the purity of Creation:

²³ Ye shall not make with me gods of silver, neither shall ye make unto you gods of gold.
²⁴ An altar of earth thou shalt make unto me, and shalt sacrifice thereon thy burnt offerings, and thy peace offerings, thy sheep and thine oxen: in all places where I record my name I will come unto thee, and I will bless thee.
²⁵ And if thou wilt make me an altar of stone, thou shalt not build it of hewn stone: for if thou lift thy tool upon it, thou has polluted it.

Exodus 20:23–25
King James version

Of course we don't like to believe we pollute things just by laying our human hands on them, or that we are evil from birth, any more than we are happy with those lines from Ecclesiastes that tell us there is a time to kill, to hate, to make war. As Friends we believe that the Spirit resides in each of us, just as in the rest of Creation. But the reality of it is, killing and hatred and the making of war—as well as the ability to love—have been part of human behavior for as far back as we can remember, and they are part of the pattern we are given to deal with. And the exchanging of one life for another is part of the pattern of Creation: the lion *does* eat the lamb, and the adder uses its poison to get food and protect itself from harm. If we are to trying to make the kind of deep changes required of us, we must accept all facets of what we are, and realize with the greatest humility that we do not understand how it all fits together.

In the Old Testament, King Solomon is considered the wisest man, and God is very pleased that Solomon asks for wisdom: *"God gave Solomon very great wisdom..."* [1 Kings 4:29–34], which included not only his famous ability to judge, but also artistic skills, (such as the ability to create songs and proverbs, and knowledge of nature).

[33] *He would speak of trees, from the cedar that is in the Lebanon to the hyssop that grows in the wall; he would speak of animals, and birds, and reptiles, and fish.*

How do we develop Earth wisdom, the wisdom given to Solomon? One definition of humility is "the ability to become teachable." We have made the assumption that we know everything, that our culture has all the answers, can fix anything that's broken. As we face the results of our actions—in the form of disintegrating societies and deteriorating ecosystems—an important step is to accept our ignorance, and become teachable. Job put it this way:

> *7 ...ask now the beasts and they shall teach thee; and the birds of the air, and they shall tell thee;*
> *8 Or speak to the earth, and it shall instruct thee; and the fishes of the sea shall declare unto thee.*
>
> Job 12:7–8

We would all do well to simply to go out among other beings, and "be teachable." Proverbs reminds us of the lessons we can learn from the other "people":

> *6 Go to the ant, you lazybones; consider its ways, and be wise.*
> *7 Without having any chief or officer or ruler,*
> *8 it prepares its food in summer, and gathers its sustenance in harvest.*
>
> Proverbs 6:6–8

> *24 Four things on the earth are small yet they are exceedingly wise:*
> *25 the ants are a people without strength, yet they provide their food in summer;*
> *26 the badgers are a people without power, yet they make their homes in the rocks;*
> *27 the locusts have no king, yet all of them march in rank;*
> *28 the lizard can be grasped in the hand, yet it is found in kings' palaces.*
>
> Proverbs 30:24–28

Jesus tells his disciples, as they go to cure and preach, to *"be as wise as serpents and as innocent as doves"* [Matthew 10:16] (this is the only time snakes get good press in the Bible, I think!). In this century, Aldo Leopold has said we must learn "to think like a mountain."

How much do we humans really know? I don't even mean knowledge of the spiritual world, of which most of us have only very brief glimpses, but of the physical world. As we go about our modern lives, do we truly have any idea of our effect on other beings? Or the effect of other beings on our lives? Do we understand the comings and goings of water, and how the soil is formed? Do we listen to the rocks and the wind and the sea?

There are about 1,413,000 species of organisms known at the present time (by "known" I mean given an official scientific name). More than half of these are insects; a little over a quarter are plants, protists, algae, fungi, bacteria, and viruses; and less than a quarter are all the other animals. Of these named species, over 99 percent are known only by a scientific name, as a voucher specimen in a museum somewhere, and maybe through an article in a scientific journal describing the organism's basic anatomy. How they function in ecosystems, how they relate to one another, and how they might relate to our species, *Homo sapiens,* is not known. And we are speaking here of *named* organisms; scientists estimate that there are at least 10 million species on the planet, and maybe as many as 100 million.

Three-quarters of the known biological world is made up of insects and plants, a riotous diversity of shapes and sizes and colors and habits. And their effects on one another, and on the soil, are beyond measure. E. O. Wilson, a Harvard biologist, tells us:

> *So important are insects and other land-dwelling arthropods that if all were to disappear, humanity probably could not last more than a few months.*

> *Most of the amphibians, reptiles, birds, and mammals would crash to extinction about the same time. Next would go the bulk of the flowering plants and with them the physical structure of most forests and other terrestrial habitats of the world. The land surface would literally rot. As dead vegetation piled up and dried out, closing the channels of the nutrient cycles, other complex forms of vegetation would die off, and with them all but a few remnants of the land vertebrates. The free-living fungi, after enjoying a population explosion of stupendous proportions, would decline precipitously, and most species would perish. The land would return to approximately its condition in early Paleozoic times, covered by mats of recumbent wind-pollinated vegetation, sprinkled with clumps of small trees and bushes here and there, largely devoid of animal life.*
>
> The Diversity of Life, 1992

I tell you this not as a gloom-and-doom scenario—for if any group survives the thoughtlessness of human actions, it will be the insects—but to share with you how little we know. I would guess that most people in America can probably tell you a great deal about the romantic lives of many movie and television personalities, but probably could not go into their own yards and show you ten insects or plants they feel they know in some way. We take an interest in that which we feel touches us, and somehow we have gotten ourselves into a massive state of denial about how the rest of Creation touches our lives.

One week in the summer of 1996, *Newsweek* magazine had its usual spread of articles—the Middle East, the upcoming Olympics in Atlanta, the Presidential race, four pages on the renewed interest in UFOs, a two-page spread on the hottest new male movie star, a page on a former football hero. And buried somewhere in all this was a little boxed article about the decline in the honeybee population, noting that the loss of the honeybees, which are the major pollinators for many of our food crops, "may threaten the food supply." Ho-hum. What was probably the most significant thing reported in the entire magazine, received only a few words of very shallow coverage.

We live in vast ignorance of *everything*, from cell functioning to the way our bodies work, from the interactions of organisms in ecosystems to the way all the living and non-living components of this planet function as that entity some call *Gaia*, our physical home, the Earth. There is not a person living—from the most learned academic scientist to the wisest farmer—who could tell you even the names of all the organisms in a cubic foot of soil, much less explain their interrelationships. And yet we continue blithely down the road called "progress," incredibly blind to that ignorance.

As Friends, we are aware of how important it is to be open to the voice of the Spirit. As we seek to learn, to listen to the non-human world as well the human world, to "think like a mountain," we might want to remember the words of Sir Thomas Browne[1]:

> *If thou could'st empty all thyself of self,*
> *Like to a shell dishabited,*
> *Then might He find thee on the ocean shelf,*
> *And say, "This is not dead,"*

---

[1] Sir Thomas Browne (1605–1682) was a 17th century British physician and essayist.

And fill thee with Himself instead.
But thou art all replete with very thou
And hast such shrewd activity,
That when He comes He says, "This is enow
Unto itself—'twere better let it be,
It is so small and full, there is no room for me."

It is very easy, as we all know, to become bogged down in our human doings, in the busyness of life and the insular nature of the modern world, and forget that we are but a part of Creation. And in the polarization that has exemplified much of what is known as the environmental movement, it has been all too easy to forget to listen to our fellow human beings as well.

"But where shall wisdom be found? And where is the place of understanding?" [Job 28:12]. Humility alone won't do it, for that can lead to paralysis, the belief that you, by yourself, can do nothing. Knowledge alone won't do it; you may be able to recite the scientific names of thousands of organisms, but that knowledge is meaningless if it is not infused first with humility, then with understanding. And the understanding of knowledge may be far from using that understanding wisely. I believe that true wisdom is found only when humility, knowledge, and understanding are infused with love. And right action comes only through affection, not a sticky sentimentality for cute Panda bears and darling dolphins, but a clear, penetrating love of the Creator and what we have been given, in its entirety: slime molds and adolescence, poison ivy and bullbrier, butterflies and backaches, mosquitos and swans—all the wondrous facets of this Creation.

¹ *If I speak in the tongues of mortals and of angels, but do not have love, I am a noisy gong or a clanging cymbal.*
² *And if I have prophetic powers, and understand all mysteries and all knowledge, and if I have all faith, so as to remove mountains, but do not have love, I am nothing.*
³ *If I give away all my possessions, and if I hand over my body to be burned so that I may boast, but do not have love, I gain nothing.*
⁴ *Love is patient; love is kind; love is not envious or boastful or arrogant or rude.*
⁵ *It does not insist on its own way; it is not irritable or resentful;*
⁶ *it does not rejoice in wrongdoing, but rejoices in the truth.*
⁷ *It bears all things, believes all things, hopes all things, endures all things.*
⁸ *Love never ends. But as for prophecies, they will come to an end; as for tongues, they will cease; as for knowledge, it will come to an end.*
⁹ *For we know only in part, and we prophecy only in part;*
¹⁰ *but when the complete comes, the partial will come to an end.*
¹¹ *When I was a child, I spoke like a child, I thought like a child, I reasoned like a child; when I became an adult, I put an end to childish ways.*
¹² *For now we see in a mirror, dimly, but then we will see face to face. Now I know only in part, then I will know fully, even as I have been known fully.*
¹³ *And now faith, hope, and love abide, these three; and the greatest of these is love.*

1 Corinthians 13

*For as in one body we have many members,
and not all the members have the same function,
so we, who are many, are one body in Christ,
and individually we are members of one another.*
Romans 12:4–5

3. Connections

Thou shalt love thy neighbor as thyself.
Matthew 22:39

[36] *Master, which is the great commandment in the law?*
[37] *Jesus said unto him, "Thou shalt love the Lord thy God with all thy heart, and with all thy soul, and with all thy mind.*
[38] *This is the first and great commandment.*
[39] *And the second is like unto it, Thou shalt love thy neighbor as thyself.*
[40] *On these two commandments hang all the law and the prophets."*
Matthew 22:36–40

The Bible tells us a great deal about neighborliness. Six of the ten commandments deal with being a good neighbor:

[12] *Honor your father and your mother, so that your days may be long in the land that the Lord your God is giving you.*
[13] *You shall not murder.*
[14] *You shall not commit adultery.*
[15] *You shall not steal.*

[16] *You shall not bear false witness against your neighbor.*
[17] *You shall not covet your neighbor's house; you shall not covet your neighbor's wife, nor his manservant, nor his maidservant, nor his ox, nor his ass, nor any thing that is your neighbor's.*

Exodus 20:12–17

Jesus puts it very simply:

In everything do to others as you would have them do to you....

Matthew 7:12

Who *is* our neighbor? Is it the family next door? The people across the street The folks in our community? Our state? Our country? In China or Guam or Costa Rica?

Once again, scripture makes clear that it takes the broad view:

[1] *Happy are those who consider the poor, the Lord delivers them in the day of trouble.*
[2] *The Lord protects them and keeps them alive; they are called happy in the land.*

Psalm 41:1–2

And Jeremiah warns:

Woe to him who builds his house by unrighteousness, and his upper room by injustice; who makes his neighbor work for nothing, and who does not give them their wages.

Jeremiah 22:13

Quakers have had a pretty good grasp from the beginning of just who our human neighbors are. But now we are being asked: are just people our neighbors?

On a very basic, physical level, each of us is a community of organisms, hosting a normal flora of bacteria, mites, roundworms, and other organisms. A few have been around so long they're integral parts of our cells; the mitochondria, scientists believe, were originally symbiotic bacteria. Some members of our body community are important in helping to keep out detrimental organisms; others are free-loaders, and a few become troublesome occasionally. There are also plenty of other organisms that would like to join this community—such as lice, ticks, fleas, fungi, viruses—and do so whenever the opportunity permits. This idea makes some people uncomfortable, for we like to think we are quite independent entities, with distinct boundaries between Us and Them.

And of course the community that is our body interacts physically with other communities, taking in food from plants and other animals, getting rid of wastes that are utilized by the detritus community. And finally, at death, our body community becoming a part of myriad other communities. If you think about it, there *are* no boundaries between one organism and another, between "life" and "non-life." We are constantly flowing from one to another: One moment a skin cell is a portion of a human being, the next moment it is part of a dust pile; then it is transformed into a house plant or a rhododendron bush; then it becomes oxygen to be breathed in by a possum, whose wastes feed bacteria that bring nutrients to an oak tree, which feeds a gypsy moth. All through the food web and the non-living world we travel, zillions of fragments are forever being put together and taken apart to make yet more unique creations.

Physically we possess no true boundaries; we are forever re-molded and recast into new forms.

Francis Hole, a soil scientist and poet (and Friend), has said, "Our bodies are disposable, biodegradable containers for spirit." We are worms and granite, oak trees and robins, sea spume and mica; we are stardust...we are each as old as the universe.

Listen to the words of poet William Carlos Williams:

> *There is nothing to eat*
> *seek it where you will,*
> *but the body of the Lord.*
> *The blessed plants*
> *and the sea, yield it*
> *to the imagination*
> *Intact.*

The Koran tells us:

Whithersoever ye turn, there is the face of God.

II:115

How do we nurture an understanding of our connections with one another, with our human community and with our non-human neighbors? The first step in getting to know other people is to look them in the eye, to recognize them. An African greeting—used for both humans and non-humans—is, *"I see you, O I see you!"* Once we have seen, we learn a name, for if we don't name, life quickly becomes very complicated (*"Hello, I'd like to speak to that person in your department who is very tall, has gray hair, a funny chin, and laughs a lot"* or *"Doctor, I think you should use that plant that's green, has fuzzy stems, purple flowers, and the bees like it...."*).

But of course, seeing and naming are only the beginning of the relationship. And naming can certainly be a two-edged sword! Look at the wars that human beings have fought, essentially over the name of God. As if we had any clue at all what "God's" true name is! As if we, with our imaginations limited by brain structure, language, and culture, could ever name or even begin to define that which is unnameable and unknowable, certainly far beyond pitiful human concepts of race and tribe and gender!

If you are to truly know another being, you must be open to learning on many levels. Marge Piercy writes:

> *I live among people who think that analyzing something is an action, who think that if they have dissected why they have done something that makes it permissible to do it again, who think that a label gives possession, that when they have identified a sharp-shinned hawk they know something of hawkness—wooing high in the air and sinking with talons locked, swooping on live prey and tasting the fresh blood spurt hot, feeling with each extended feather the warm and cold shift of the winds and the sculpture of the invisible masses of moving air. Dealing in words, I try to remember how far they go and where they leave off. Hungry for food for my brain, I try to remember all the other ways of knowing that coexist.*
>
> Braided Lives, 1982

We gain this kind of knowing through one of the greatest gifts the Creator has given humanity, our imaginations. Wendell Berry (1993) notes: "It is by imagination that we cross over the differences between ourselves and other beings and thus learn compassion, forbearance, mercy, forgiveness, sympathy, and love—the virtues without which neither we nor the world can live."

Another keen observer, Loren Eiseley, writes of standing on the edge of a pond and seeing a frog:

Whenever I catch a frog's eye... I stand quite still and try hard not to move or lift a hand since it would only frighten him. And standing thus it finally comes to me that this is the most enormous extension of vision of which life is capable: the projection of itself into other lives. This is the magnificent power of humanity. It is, far more than any spatial adventure, the supreme epitome of the reaching out.

The Immense Journey, 1946

Friend John Woolman[1] wrote very movingly of an experience he had as a child, an experience which helped him make the imaginative leap to understanding:

I may mention a remarkable circumstance that occurred in my childhood. On going to a neighbor's house, I saw on the way a robin sitting on her nest, and as I came near she went off; but having young ones, she flew about, and with many cries expressed her concern for them. I stood and threw stones at her, and one striking her, she fell down dead. At first I was pleased with the exploit, but after a few

---

[1] John Woolman (1720–1772) is considered to be one of the great Quaker "saints," a man whose efforts to lead a life of integrity still stand as a shining example. He is best known for his witness against slavery.

> *minutes was seized with horror, at having, in a sportive way, killed an innocent creature while she was careful for her young.*
>
> *I beheld her lying dead, and thought those young ones, for which she was so careful, must now perish for want of their dam to nourish them. After some painful considerations on the subject, I climbed up the tree, took all the young birds, and killed them, supposing that better than to leave them to pine away and die miserably. In this case I believe that Scripture proverb was fulfilled, "The tender mercies of the wicked are cruel." I then went on my errand, and for some hours could think of little else but the cruelties I had committed, and was much troubled. Thus He whose tender mercies are over all his works hath placed a principle in the human mind, which incites to exercise goodness towards every living creature; and this being singly attended to, people become tender-hearted and sympathizing; but when frequently and totally rejected, the mind becomes shut up in a contrary disposition.*
>
> The Journal of John Woolman, pp. 2–3
Whittier edition

I am fortunate that every few years I am able to accompany my husband Mark to Jamaica, where he teaches a course in Tropical Ecology. Each morning, weather permitting, we are out on the reefs snorkeling, gazing in wonder and delight at the amazing coral reef community. Because I swim without a wet suit—in only a bathing suit covered with T-shirt so I don't burn in the sun—I am in direct contact with the water. It is a place "fearfully and wonderfully made," a community of bright colors and quick fishy dartings, of waving anemones and fiery coral, of gentle sea slugs and gleaming barracuda, of spiny sea urchins and pulsing jellyfish. And in rare moments, after I've been there a little while, I feel as if I belong. I forget I am a guest and become, however fleetingly, a member of that community. And it is always with a sense of shock—and loss—that I realize I must rise to the surface and become again an air-breathing creature.

When we are in contact like this—when we truly connect—we know these moments as precious. Awe, gratitude, and joy all spring from within us when we are connected. Meeting for Worship can connect us; being in non-human communities can connect us; dance, music, sex, good food, prayer, a long conversation with a good friend, laughter, tears—all can connect us. And they are *all* "natural"—there are really no natural-versus-unnatural connections; there are just *connections*, an unlimited number of ways to be one with Creation and the Creator.

Where we fail is in not allowing true "connections" to occur. We disconnect ourselves at every interval, by our fanatical adherence to rigid time frames, by choosing the making of money over connections with family and friends, or by watching endless hours of television—that great disconnector which turns us into observers *of* rather than participants *in* life. We disconnect in our culture's emphasis on doing things faster rather than better; in our need to categorize people by their gender or race or religion or nationality; in the eating of packaged and processed food that often bears little resemblance to the plants and animals that yielded their substance for them. ...The disconnections seem endless.

For me, personally, one of the symbols of our culture's disconnectedness comes through music. Several years ago I spent three weeks with a group of American teenagers in a village in Estonia. Our Estonian hosts gave us a wonderful Fourth of July party, and after we ate we sat around a bonfire and sang. The Estonian teenagers would sing a song, and then the Americans. The Estonians sang beautiful folk songs, in four-part harmony. The American teenagers, to my great surprise (for I grew up singing) knew very few songs they were able to sing: although they knew the words to many popular songs, such as music of the Beatles, they were not able to sing them. They suggested songs such as "A hundred bottles of beer on the wall"! I have attended high school graduations where the students could barely sing the class song they had *practiced*. I've even heard singing recently, on television and in the movies, that barely passed for music, in sharp contrast to movies of just thirty or forty years ago. In my heart, this musical disharmony is a clear symbol of the disconnectedness and disharmony of our modern life.

Much of what's called "New Age" spirituality seems to be about people's deep desire to reconnect. I know that many people object to New Age philosophies; to crystals, herbs, incense and other paraphernalia; to what they fear is pagan worship; to the growing interest in Native American, Buddhist, or other non-Judeo-Christian spiritualities. At the core of this movement, however, seems to be a desire to reconnect with the pattern of Creation. And with so many seeking in those directions, what does this say about traditional, mainstream churches, where many feel they do *not* find those connections with Creation? While fussing about "New Agers," have traditional churches forgotten to take a good look in the mirror? I wonder whether Jesus might once again say:

> [23] *Woe to you, scribes and Pharisees, hypocrites! For you tithe mint, dill, and cumin, and have neglected the weightier matters of the law: justice and mercy and faith. It is these you ought to have practiced without neglecting the others.*
> [24] *You blind guides! You strain out a gnat but swallow a camel!*
>
> Matthew 23:23–24

To really know something—and to truly love it—you must feel yourself connected to it, in a very personal way. The more abstract you make the connection, the less real care you will give it. It's like the difference between writing a check to a charity, and visiting with a sick friend. Both may be helpful, but the abstract act of writing a check to help those you have never known will never have the affection of personal contact. It is said that "familiarity breeds contempt," and on a superficial level that is true: the better you know someone, the better you know their faults and limitations. But I think more often than not, familiarity breeds affection, the sense that you know and are known, warts and all, and still cherish and are cherished. And familiarity enables you to recognize that each member of a community has a role and offers unique gifts.

In his letter to the Romans, Paul writes:

> [4] *For as in one body we have many members, and not all the members have the same function,*

⁵ so we, who are many, are one body in Christ, and individually we are members one of another.
⁶ We have gifts that differ according to the grace given to us; prophecy, in proportion to faith;
⁷ ministry, in ministering; the teacher, in teaching;
⁸ the exhorter, in exhortation; the giver, in generosity; the leader, in diligence; the compassionate, in cheerfulness.
Romans 12:4–8

What happens when the community suffers the loss of a member? What happens when a neighbor dies? When biologists have bemoaned the great loss of species we are experiencing, some have accused them of simply mourning change itself. After all, the line goes, change is inevitable, which of course is true. But today we are speaking of a new kind of change, the like of which has never before occurred on this scale, in this time frame. And when we mourn this change, we are not talking of grief over the loss of a beloved relative or friend, whose passing we mourn but whose presence among us we also celebrate. No, I speak of the loss of a kind that will never be resurrected and whose passing will be noted consciously by few. I speak of deaths with no funerals; I speak of extinctions. Who speaks for these dead? Who sings a lament when the last member of a species is gone? And who understands the few mourners at the wake?

Aldo Leopold, writing of the passing of the Passenger Pigeon in his book, *A Sand County Almanac*, wrote: "For one species to mourn the death of another is a new thing under the sun. The Cro-Magnon who slew the last mammoth thought only of steaks. The sailor who clubbed the last auk thought of nothing at all. But we, who have lost our pigeons, mourn the loss."

Do you understand the pain of those in Bosnia, seeing their loved ones slaughtered and their villages destroyed? Have you heard the cries from Rwanda, as Hutu and Tutsi battle one another? Surely we have all grieved over the senseless deaths in these and so many places where human madness has won out over human kindness. Can you then not hear the sound of ecosystems dying, the cry of thousands of species looking for members of their communities, which are no longer?

In Ramah there was a voice heard, lamentation and weeping, and great mourning, Rachel weeping for her children, and would not be comforted, because they were not.
Matthew 2:18

That there are mourners there is no question. The grief comes tentatively, personally. "Where is the Indigo Bunting I used to see on the telephone wires every summer over by the Johnson farm?" "Did you hear a Whip-Poor-Will this summer—we never heard one at our place?" "I haven't seen a Luna Moth in years." And there are other questions, bravely framed as scientific inquiry, but secretly as laments: "Have you noticed there seem to be far fewer shells on the beaches?" "Are the number of snakes declining in the state?" "Doesn't it seem to you that there are fewer insects?"

I believe the need to mourn what's being lost is crucial. The loss of a warbler song in May, or the destruction of a favorite meadow, are personal losses. The grief is essential, and to deny it is to keep a wound festering. But society at large does not recognize the dying, and therefore rejects the need to mourn, under the guise that the mourner is merely lamenting "progress." And the grief is deepened, I think, knowing we are both mourner and murderer, the bereaved as well as the executioner. "I am become Death," were Oppenheimer's words, I believe, when he witnessed the first atomic bomb explosion. Does it not feel at times that *we* "are become death," we, our culture and our diseased ways?

The Creator felt that way about people at one time, so disgusted with the whole lot of us that God decided to destroy Creation:

> [13] *And God said to Noah, "I have determined to make an end of all flesh, for the earth is filled with violence because of them; now I am going to destroy them along with the earth."*
>
> Genesis 6:13

But God realized there *were* righteous people, and decided to save part of Creation, and start anew, reestablishing the covenant with the people and with all living things.

> [11] *I establish my covenant with you, that never again shall all flesh be cut off by the waters of a flood, and never again shall there be a flood to destroy the earth.*
> [12] *This is the sign of the covenant that I make between me and you and every living creature that is with you, for all future generations.*
> [13] *I shall set my bow in the clouds, and it shall be a sign of the covenant between me and the earth.*
>
> Genesis 9:11–13

God decided that Creation was worth saving, and that human beings were—and are—part of that Creation. If the Creator can forgive us—and is that not the entire message of the New Testament?—Does that not give us great hope? The world will not be a better place without people—although in our collective guilt we sometimes feel that way—but the world *will* be a better place when people learn to live in right relationship to the rest of Creation.

As Quakers, we are keenly aware that to be full human beings, we must recognize the full humanity of all other people. But I think that each of us will be fully human only when we recognize the full Aliveness of all Creation, and act on that recognition, when we learn to "speak to that of God in Everything," and to humbly admit our dependence upon that great Web we call Creation. Hear the words of Old Jack, an elderly farmer in one of Wendell Berry's novels :

The way we are we are members of each other. All of us. Everything. The difference ain't in who is a member and who is not, but in who knows it and who don't.

The Wild Birds, 1986

The effect of righteousness will be peace, and the result of righteousness, quietness and trust forever.
Isaiah 32:17

4. Right Relationship

> *For where your treasure is,*
> *there will your heart be also.*
> Matthew 6:21

You see, I am alive.
You see, I stand in good relation to the earth.
You see, I stand in good relation to the gods.
You see, I stand in good relation to all that is beautiful.
You see, I stand in good relation to you.
You see, I am alive, I am alive.

This Native American poem expresses the joy of living in balance, in right relationship to the Creator, to other people, and to all Creation. What does it mean to stand in good relation to the Earth? In good relation to all that is beautiful? In good relation to one another?

Are we standing in good relation to the Earth? Here are a few of the facts:

- Each second a forested area the size of a football field is cut down; we lose an area a little smaller than the state of Kentucky each year.[1]

- Billions of tons of topsoil are lost from cropland each year. As the quality of agricultural land diminishes with topsoil loss, there are also decreasing water supplies available for irrigation and increasing conversion of farmland industry and other forms of development. World grain production in 1995 was 5 percent below the 1990 harvest, and carryover stocks declined.[2]
- The increase in CO_2 and the concentration of other gases in the atmosphere may cause as much as a 5- to 7-degree Fahrenheit rise in mean global temperature by the year 2040; this is as much change in mean global temperature as has occurred since the last ice age, but it will occur in 50 years rather than in 20,000. 1997 was the warmest year on record; the ten warmest years of the past 130 years occurred during the 1980s and 1990s.[3]
- Air pollution damages crops, livestock, human health, and ecosystems all over the world. "What goes up, must come down": the pollution that comes from one place ends up in another. Soot from the oil fires in Kuwait made the snows in the Himalayas black and oily; the fallout from the Chernobyl nuclear power plant disaster fell on Sweden and Norway. There has been a 40-percent increase in the asthma rate in the industrialized Western world since 1982, and one-third of the victims are children. Air pollution, both indoor and outdoor, is considered to be the major factor.[4]
- The release of chlorofluorocarbons (CFCs) in the atmosphere is breaking down the ozone layer, which protects us from ultraviolet radiation; there are concerns that this will affect both agriculture and human health.

- Thousands of barrels of toxic and radioactive waste have been buried in landfills or dumped into the ocean; these are time bombs for future generations.
- Each year, three million children under age five die of diarrheal diseases,[5] related to poor water quality, a direct result of poverty and the unequal distribution of the world's resources.
- The human population reached 5.8 billion in 1996, and is predicted to reach nearly 10 billion by the year 2050[6]; at the same time, the planet will be facing major changes in climate, with unprecedented effects on agriculture and coastal habitations. The ongoing loss of topsoil will act in synergy to have an impact on the human ability to produce food.
- Current estimates suggest that each hour anywhere from four to eight species go extinct (compare this to the "massive" die-off of the dinosaurs, which occurred at a rate of one species every 1,000 years). We believe that by the year 2000, 20 percent of all existing species will be gone from the wild (the tiger and the rhinoceros likely to be among them). We have named only a small percentage of these species and know very little about how they function within their ecosystems. Some scientists have likened most species to rivets in a jet: you don't see them, or think about them, but they are crucial. How many rivets can a jet lose before it crashes? How many species can be lost before ecosystems crash, with unpredictable effects on all life on the planet, including human life?

Okay—enough. We have been bombarded with such facts for many years now. I first saw Mark, my such facts for many years now. I first saw Mark, my future husband, at an organizational meeting for the first celebration of Earth Day at the University of Rhode Island in 1970; in 1995, at the 25th anniversary celebration of Earth Day, we were still saying the same things. And amazingly, they have been said, in some form, for thousands of years! I have already mentioned many Bible passages that talk about God's laws for protecting the Creation. But God also gave some clear instructions on how to be in right relationship with the land itself, through laws that required a year of rest for cultivated land every seven years:

> *Six years you shall sow your field, and six years you shall prune your vineyard, and gather in their yield; but in the seventh year there shall be a sabbath of complete rest for the land, a sabbath for the Lord; you shall not sow your field or prune your vineyard.*
>
> Leviticus 25:3–4

There was also to be a year of rest every 50th year, the jubilee, when all slaves were to be freed and land leases would expire, everyone returning to their ancestral holdings and their families. God says quite firmly that people cannot own the land forever:

> [23] *The land shall not be sold in perpetuity, for the land is mine; with me you are but aliens and tenants.*
> [24] *Throughout the land that you hold, you shall provide for the redemption of the land.*
>
> Leviticus 25:23–24

And the Bible tells us, in quite clear terms, what will happen if we don't follow God's laws, including our covenant relationship with the land, in these lines from Leviticus:

¹⁹ *I will break your proud glory, and I will make your sky like iron and your earth like copper.*
²⁰ *Your strength shall be spent to no purpose: your land shall not yield its produce, and the trees of the land shall not yield their fruit.*
³³ *And you I will scatter among the nations, and I will unsheath the sword against you; your land shall be a desolation, and your cities a waste.*
³⁴ *Then the land shall make up for its sabbath years as long as it lies desolate, while you are in the hands of your enemies, then the land shall rest and make up for its sabbath years.*
³⁵ *As long as it lies desolate, it shall have the rest it did not have on your sabbaths when you were living on it.*
Leviticus 26:19–20; 33–35

Proverbs also reminds us of the land relationship:

²⁰ *Therefore walk in the way of the good, and keep to the paths of the just.*
²¹ *For the upright will abide in the land and the innocent will remain in it;*
²² *but the wicked will be cut off from the land, and the treacherous will be rooted out of it.*
Proverbs 2:20–22

Of course Isaiah has something to say on this:

⁴ *The earth dries up and withers, the world languishes and withers, the heavens languish together with the earth.*
⁵ *The earth lies polluted under its inhabitants; for they have transgressed laws, violated the statutes, broken their everlasting covenant.*

⁶ *Therefore a curse devours the earth, and its inhabitants suffer for their guilt.*

Isaiah 24:4–13

as does Hosea:

For they sow the wind, and they shall reap the whirlwind.

Hosea 8:7

Apparently these laws involving land redemption were mostly ignored by the Israelites from the beginning (Metzger and Murphy 1991). Ever since then, it's curious how little we have heard from the religious community about the Levitical laws involving the sabbath for the land, and the fact that the land ultimately belongs to God, while other Levitical laws, such as those against homosexuality, have been widely trumpeted.

Is this a case of selective vision? How easy it is to attack a practice when we believe it has nothing to do with us, but oh how scary things get when our money is involved, and how contorted the denial becomes! We have people in our country who will not admit that the actions they take on "their" land affect adjoining lands and waters (or perhaps they simply do not care about those effects). Can you imagine what might happen if the religious community were to begin to preach about sabbath for the land? Decades of "cold war" taught us how terrified capitalist society is at the idea of communal land ownership, and the failure of industrial communism informs us that different models are needed. There is much new thinking to be done, for the area of private property rights—and our culture's belief that it can take endlessly from the Earth—need all the spirit-led thought and action they can muster.

Wendell Berry in *Home Economics* (1987) states: "The industrial mind is a mind without compunction; it simply accepts that people, ultimately, will be treated as things and that things, ultimately, will be treated as garbage."

Even if you've never read the Bible, you couldn't have helped but know, as part of our culture, that the Bible is ambivalent about wealth. Solomon and Job, for example, are rewarded with great wealth, but those who let the pursuit of wealth become the driving force in their lives are warned over and over again. How familiar to all of us are these lines from Scripture:

[9] *But those who want to be rich fall into temptation and are trapped by many senseless and harmful desires that plunge people into ruin and destruction.*

[10] *For the love of money is a root of all kinds of evil, and in their eagerness to be rich, some have wandered away from the faith and pierced themselves with many pains.*

1 Timothy 6:9–10

[19] *Lay not up for yourselves treasures upon earth, where moth and rust dost corrupt, and where thieves break through and steal:*

[20] *But lay up for yourselves treasures in heaven, where neither moth nor rust doth corrupt, and where thieves do not break through nor steal:*

[21] *For where your treasure is, there will your heart be also.*

[24] *No man can serve two masters: for either he will hate the one, and love the other, or else he will hold to the one, and despise the other. Ye cannot serve God and mammon.*

Matthew 6:19–24

> *It is easier for a camel to go through the eye of a needle than for a rich man to enter the kingdom of heaven.*
>
> Mark 10:25

Nor are admonitions about loving money only to be found in the New Testament:

> ¹⁵ *The idols of the nations are silver and gold, the work of human hands.*
> ¹⁶ *They have mouths, but they do not speak; they have eyes but they do not see;*
> ¹⁷ *they have ears, but they do not hear, and there is not breath in their mouths.*
> ¹⁸ *Those who make them and all who trust them shall become like them.*
>
> Psalm 135:15–18

> *The lover of money will not be satisfied with money; nor the lover of wealth, with gain.*
>
> Ecclesiastes 5:10

> *You have sown much, and harvested little; you eat, but you never have enough; you drink, but you never have your fill; you clothe yourselves, but no one is warm; and you that earn wages earn wages to put them into a bag with holes.*
>
> Haggai 1:6

The entire Bible is a treatise about right relationship, warning over and over about the sins of excess wealth, lust, power, and religious apostasy. The Old Testament is full of God telling people how to behave, explaining over and over that God *expects* responsible behavior—and of the people ignoring the laws and being repeatedly punished. The New Testament is about the Divine Spirit coming to earth and showing people how it's done, trying to capture their imaginations in a totally new way... and people are still ignoring God's message.

John Woolman was very concerned about right relationship with wealth, and right relationship among people:

> *...Look, my dear friends, to Divine Providence, and follow in simplicity that exercise of body, that plainness and frugality, which true wisdom leads to; so may you be preserved from those dangers... such as are aiming at outward ease and greatness.*
>
> *Treasures, though small, attained on a true principle of virtue, are sweet; and while we walk in the light of the Lord there is true comfort and satisfaction in the possession; neither the murmurs of an oppressed people, nor a throbbing, uneasy conscience, nor anxious thoughts about the events of things, hinder the enjoyment of them.*
>
> The Journal of John Woolman, 1961

Notice that Woolman is talking about the ability to enjoy life to the fullest, when we are in right relationship with our possessions.

Woolman recalls in his *Journal* a discussion with a Friend who was defending the slave trade, saying it was a biblical imperative that the descendants of Cain, whom God made black in punishment for killing Abel, be enslaved:

> *...I was troubled to perceive the darkness of their imaginations, and in some pressure of spirit said, "The love of ease and gain are the motives in general of keeping slaves, and men are wont to take hold of weak arguments to support a cause which is*

> *unreasonable. I have no interest on either side, save only the interest which I desire to have in the truth. I believe liberty is their right, and as I see they are not only deprived of it, but treated in other respects with inhumanity in many places, I believe He who is a refuge for the oppressed will, in his own time, plead their cause, and happy will it be for such as walk in uprightness before him."*

As Woolman traveled throughout the eastern United States during the mid-1700s in witness against slavery, he worried about the effect of slavery on both the slave and the enslaver. He wrote in his journal:

> *...the white people and their children so generally [live] without much labour.... I saw in these southern provinces so many vices and corruptions increased by this trade and this way of life, that it appeared to me as a dark gloominess hanging over the land; and though now many willingly run into it, yet in [the] future the consequences will be grievous to posterity.*

Should *we* hear "the murmurs of an oppressed people" or have "a throbbing uneasy conscience" as we go about our lives? Well, do we know where our electricity comes from? Do we know if people have been forced off their lands, deprived of their hunting grounds, and seen their cultures disintegrate so that we here in America can forget to turn out the lights? Do we know where our garbage goes—whose community it is buried in or who breathes the smoke from the incinerator where it is burned? Do we know whose impoverished country accepts the toxic wastes we refuse to have on American soil? It seems to me we continue to make that age-old assumption that "has proved to be ruinous beyond measure: the assumption that it is permissible to ruin one place or culture for the sake of another" [Berry 1993].

So we continue to struggle with "the love of ease and gain," both in our relationship with our fellow human beings and our relationship to the rest of Creation. We reap the bitter fruits of slavery even now, 130 years after its abolishment; how long will we reap the fruits of our treatment of the Earth? Friends are very proud of Quaker achievements in helping to right our relationship with the slaves; to hear some Friends, you'd think that abolition happened just yesterday and they'd been part of the Underground Railroad themselves! Let us turn around, Friends, and look into the future: In the year 2128, 130 years from now, will Friends look back so proudly at Quaker achievement in righting our relationship with Creation? What are—and will be—the spiritual consequences of our disconnection from the Earth?

Realize, Friends, that we're not trying to "preserve" the Earth! That sounds like we're going to pickle it, put it neatly in a jar and keep it on a museum shelf somewhere, to be dusted off and gawked at every now and then. *That's* how we've been treating the Earth for far too long—as "other." The Earth will likely do quite nicely preserving itself—we're trying to save *ourselves,* by bringing ourselves back into right relationship with Creation and the Creator.

Christ tells us:

Be ye therefore perfect, even as your Father which is in heaven is perfect.

Matthew 5:48.

I struggled with this word "perfect" for many years. I knew there was no way *I* would ever be perfect; that was simply unattainable for any person, and most certainly for me. But then a Friend in our Meeting who had studied Hebrew said that another translation for "perfect" was "whole." "Be ye whole": now *that* has potential, *that* gives us hope. What if we focus on wholeness—*holiness*—the bringing together of all earth communities?

How do we begin to create wholeness? We begin in the most obvious place, ourselves. As I mentioned in the first chapter, one area that seems to be out of right relationship in today's world is *time*. But this, too, is an old problem—look at that wonderful story of Mary and Martha that Luke tells. In the story, Jesus and the disciples are traveling:

> *Now as they went on their way, he entered a certain village, where a woman named Martha welcomed him into her home. She had a sister named Mary, who sat at the Lord's feet and listened to what he was saying. But Martha was distracted by her many tasks; so she came to him and asked, "Lord, do you not care that my sister has left me to do all the work by myself? Tell her then to help me." But the Lord answered her, "Martha, Martha, you are worried and distracted by many things; there is need of only one thing. Mary has chosen the better part, which will not be taken away from her."*
>
> Luke 10:38–42

Now can't you just hear Martha muttering in the kitchen and banging pots for the next hour: "Of *course* she's got the better part; she's in there sitting on her duff while I'm in here cooking dinner for a small tribe!" What woman doesn't resonate to that story and, while fully understanding Jesus' message, still sympathize with Martha? How to balance the Mary and Martha in all our lives is crucial to coming 'round right with time!

And yet, I cannot help but wonder what Jesus might have to say about the dishonoring of Martha—of all that relates to the so-called feminine side of us in today's society. Rearing children, cooking meals, cleaning house, caring for our neighbors, tending the sick and elderly—the keeping of a home and caring for a community—are so devalued now that people who do these things full time often apologize for not "working"! Modern society has a deep prejudice against work that does not earn a wage. After all, time is money, right?

John Woolman also wrote on right relationship with time:

> *So great is the hurry in the spirit of this world, that in aiming to do business quickly and to gain wealth the creation at this day doth loudly groan.*

Woolman found ways to make clear his witness against slavery, such as wearing undyed cloth (so he would have no connection with the trade of indigo dye, which used slave labor) and refusing to write bills of sale for slaves. Today things seem more murky, it is often harder to make those clear witnesses. But how did Woolman know when he was not in right relationship? He listened to the Inner Light constantly, to assess what he should do. When he was not in right relationship, he knew it. He would be "in considerable agitation of mind." If we are to discern our place in Creation, we must also take that time to listen, to be open to that "still small voice." This is the reason I stress the need for us to get into right relationship with time.

One of my gauges for right relationship is beauty. I don't mean the way we people usually label beauty, calling a rose "beautiful" and a tarantula "ugly." I mean the true beauty of *integrity*. If something is beautiful, there is a harmony to it—it radiates wholeness, whether we speak of an animal, a plant, music, a child's toy, or a meal we serve. We know when we have had a beautiful day: the pieces fit together, and we flow from one part to another. If we live in a beautiful way, we know it. I think it is especially important that we surround children with true beauty—in our homes, our schools, our Meetings—that we envelope them with that integrity, both as a spiritual shield against the crumbling integrity of our wider society, and as a germ of hope.

Isaiah has a lovely, Quakerly phrase about what will happen when we are in right relationship:

[17] *The effect of righteousness will be peace, and the result of righteousness, quietness and trust forever.*
Isaiah 32:17

Ecclesiastes also reminds us of the beauty of the pattern, of being part of the inner stillness:

[3] *What do people gain from all the toil at which they toil under the sun?*
[4] *A generation goes, and a generation comes, but the earth remains forever.*
[5] *The sun rises and the sun goes down, and hurries to the place where it rises.*
[6] *The wind blows to the south, and goes around to the*

> *north; round and round goes the wind, and on its circuits the wind returns.*
> *⁷ All streams run to the sea, but the sea is not full; to the place where the streams flow, there they continue to flow.*
>
> Ecclesiastes 1:2–7

We know it is not easy to change our ways, our patterns of living. But I like to think that even our mistakes and backslidings have a use. The analogy of gardening came to my heart in worship one First Day—of how I need to root out bad habits, like I need to weed the garden. Some habits are like chickweed and easily uprooted; although they may pop up again from seed, they can again be removed. Others habits have deep taproots, and grubbing them out is sweaty and difficult. How easy to remove only those parts which show on the surface, and leave the deep roots to sprout again! Weeds will always pop up in any empty space, any place in the heart left neglected and untended. But I had a happy thought: The weeds can be thrown onto the compost heap of the soul, fertilizing one's life and adding richness and depth to the soil. It is from that compost that we grow.

Friends, let us keep these words in our hearts; let us allow them to grow in our imaginations as we seek the path back to right relationship:

> *You see, we are alive.*
> *You see, we stand in good relation to the earth.*
> *You see, we stand in good relation to the gods.*
> *You see, we stand in good relation to all that is beautiful.*
> *You see, we stand in good relation to each other.*
> *You see, we are alive, we are alive.*

*Love does no wrong to a neighbor;
therefore, love is the fulfilling of the law.*
Romans 13:10

5. Stewardship

What does the Lord require of thee?
Micah 6:8

A few years ago I was in Houston, Texas visiting with my sister. Now I'm a native Texan, and there are two things in the world that all Texans have to have, and one of them is cowboy boots. I thought that a good pair of cowboy boots would be useful in the plant inventory work that I sometimes do, so my sister and I headed into the wilds of downtown Houston to Sheplers, a true cowboy emporium. We wandered inside this building, resplendent with fringed shirts and dazzling bolos, and were approached by the salesman. "Well, little lady, what can I do for you?" he asked. I explained about the work I did (trying not to bristle at the "little lady"), about being in woods full of Bullbrier and Poison Ivy, often off trails, and how I thought a good practical pair of cowboy boots might be useful. He looked me up and down with a perplexed air and finally blurted out, "Are you one of them save-the-whale-ers?"

"Well, yeah, I guess so." I replied "I'm from New England. I'm a save-the-whale-er!

I abuse, starve, or murder them. Responsible parenting means helping my children to grow and become whole adults. So how in the world have we gotten the idea that dominion over the planet means to plunder it? Or that the word "subdue" necessarily means "to destroy," while it can simply mean to put land under cultivation?

How do we reconcile our actions over the centuries with the many verses in the Old Testament that stress responsible stewardship of the land? I'm aware that some people recently have also reacted to the idea of our being "stewards," with the inference that we are in charge of things. Others remind us that a steward is a type of servant; on board a ship, a steward is in charge of provisions and dining arrangements, and is definitely not the Captain! The idea that we might serve as stewards, as the ones who help take care of details, seems similar in spirit to me as the Quaker term "clerk," another word deliberately chosen to de-emphasize the "in-charge" aspects of true leadership.

Another idea that some believers appear to have drawn from Christian theology is the notion that earthly life is not important, for the goal is heavenly reward; what happens on earth doesn't really matter unless it prevents your going to heaven. The focus has been on individual spiritual salvation, not on the future well-being of the community. This focus on individual salvation enables us also to stress individual comfort and profit, which draws us farther out of community. Such ideas have evolved far from the words and deeds of the early Apostles, who stressed the importance of community, of caring for each other. Did not Peter remind the early Christians of Christ's message to *"Love your neighbor as yourself"*? Love does no wrong to a neighbor; therefore, love is the fulfilling of the law" [Romans 13:9–10].

The Medieval Christian church delineated rigid hierarchies of being, from God down through the angelic beings to Man, Woman, animals, etc., hierarchies which created polarization and boundaries. We talk of Man *versus* Nature... Day versus night... Good versus Evil... the damned versus the saved... Black versus White... Man versus Woman. In culture after culture, not just among Judeo-Christian societies, boundaries are set—boundaries based on species, gender, class, race, nationality, boundaries that enable us to treat some things with love and kindness, and others as objects for hatred, destruction, or simply mindless disregard. Always there is the idea that one thing must be better than the other, that one must conquer and the other lose. The results of this rigidity: a deteriorating global society, with violence and poverty and hatred, and deteriorating ecosystems undergoing the greatest extinction of species ever known in such a time frame.

Another common theme in our culture, and the mainstay of our economic system, is that "bigger is better," that growth can—indeed must—be unlimited. This is a curious concept I can't find elsewhere in nature: Even Redwood trees and Blue Whales have a limit on their size. Naturalist John Nichols states that "Growth for the sake of growth is the ideology of a cancer cell." But in North America we equate well-being with owning in excess: big cars, fur coats, huge homes, lots of clothes, numerous gadgets, leaving lights on, wasting water....we equate wealth with being able to own and consume in excess. It takes 25 people in some other parts of the world to utilize the amount of resources one American uses in a year. I wonder, are we 25 times happier? We need to ask, of both ourselves and everyone we know: does owning lots of possessions truly bring joy into our lives? It's that age-old question: what is enough?

I do a very simple exercise when I talk about these things with local civic groups and garden clubs. Before I begin my talk, I ask everyone to write down on a piece of paper what they hold dearest in their lives—just a word or phrase. I assure them that there's no right or wrong answer, and have them pass in the papers to me. At the end of the talk we go over them, and of course, they've all listed God, family, friends, gardens, "nature," or good health—nothing whatsoever to do with possessions.

Think for a minute about how life has changed in the past 150 years or so. Think about the good things, such as increases in longevity, lowered death rates from childbirth and epidemic disease, the ability to travel and communicate quickly over incredible distances, and the freedom from much back-breaking labor. So much of this has happened so rapidly that our culture has not had a chance to "catch up" with the changes; we accept technological changes without an understanding of their effects on our lives.

For example, we have accepted increasingly powerful cars, so we are able to go from one place to another faster and faster. This means we need more highways that can accommodate high-speed travel and more energy to fuel those cars, and that we live at a faster pace. We have accepted the rapid pace of our lives without much question—it sort of crept up on us. But now we are beginning to ask questions: What are we doing with the time we "save" getting there faster? Does increased speed compensate for the loss of land destroyed in highway construction? Does our reliance on the automobile justify the pollution it causes (and the subsequent effects on ecosystem and human health)? Does our use of an earth-extracted material (such as bauxite, to make aluminum, or petroleum, for gasoline) justify the destruction that will be required to extract it? Is high-speed travel worth the thousands of lives lost in highway accidents each year? Is driving high-speed automobiles worth the cost of wars over natural resources, such as the recent war in the Persian Gulf? We are finally beginning to ask: what really aids us in our technological world, and what just appears to? What is "appropriate technology," and what is superfluous? We *all* need to be thinking about these questions.

We need to consider the effect of technology on our social structure. As a nation of TV watchers and computer users, we seem to spend more time manipulating the technical rather than participating in the social. Simultaneously we are seeing more isolation among neighbors, more violence and fear, less stable family structure...these are problems we hear about all the time!

We seem to have forgotten the importance of relationships, the need for community, the need to feel connected to one another. And we are reminded constantly of what happens when people, both young and old, feel disconnected: Drug and alcohol abuse, crime, despair, abuse of the weak, pollution, suicide, and promiscuous sexuality are all symptoms of our disconnections, and our fear of being disconnected. Focusing on individual consumption, on owning, on "having it all," we have torn our communities apart.

And the problem is now global: For good or ill, all our cultures are touching one another. We *are* interacting, and like it or not, a large portion of the world's population has accepted, at least materially, Western ideas of progress. Remember what happened when the Iron Curtain fell: "And they all went shopping..." One young Friend said to me that we seem to be in a state of "enthusiastic decadence." We need desperately to ask: to what extent has technology empowered and enlivened us, given us joy and happiness, and to what extent has it harmed us and disconnected us from others? Can the world afford to have everyone live at the same consumption level as Americans? Or can we here in the United States learn from people in other parts of the world, people who are leading happy, healthy lives at a much lower level of consumption than we are?

I think Quakers are an ideal group to help bring some of those models to the wealthy "Western world." We might use for inspiration Luke 12:48:

> ...From everyone to whom much has been given, much will be required; and from the one to whom much has been entrusted, even more will be demanded.

We are given much, Friends, and much is now asked of us.

There is other guidance in the Bible. The New Testament's story of the dynamics of the developing

Christian community is particularly enlightening in this area. When I was young I was very bored by the books of the New Testament after the four gospels—all that bickering over who should be circumcised and whether or not you could be a Christian without being a Jew... on and on. Now that I'm approaching fifty, however, and have participated in the formation of several organizations, I feel much more tender toward this part of the Bible. The personality conflicts, the squabbling over minutiae, the endless meetings—I especially sympathize with the young man who goes to sleep and falls off a balcony after Paul has talked for hours during a meeting—fortunately Paul is there to revive him, and then goes on and talks until dawn! Sound like some meetings you've been to?

It seems to me that the enthusiasm of the new Christians as they try to spread the message Jesus brought, the mistakes they make in over-zealousness or in getting Christ's message straight, the martyrdom of those who are imprisoned or die for spreading the word—all of these have parallels in the modern peace, social justice, and environmental movements. They caution us to listen carefully and lovingly to one another, to remain open to revelation, to support one another in the face of societal disdain and persecution, and to give our all in Speaking Truth to Power.

How's this for a modern tale? In Acts 19, Paul is still in Ephesus, preaching the gospel. A silversmith named Demetrius, who makes silver statues of the goddess Artemis, hears Paul's words. He's disturbed at what he hears, so he gathers together other silver workers and notes that Paul's message could damage their business:

[27] *...Men, you know that we get our wealth from this business.*

[26] *You also see and hear that not only in Ephesus but in almost the whole of Asia this Paul has persuaded and drawn away a considerable number of people by saying that gods made with hands are not gods.*

[27] *And there is danger not only that this trade of ours may come into disrepute but also that the temple of the great goddess Artemis will be scorned, and that she will be deprived of her majesty that brought all Asia and the world to worship her.*

Acts 19:25–27

Demetrius's words stir up a near riot: For two hours people shout, *"Great is Artemis of the Ephesians!"* [Acts 19:34]. Finally everybody is calmed down by the town clerk, who points out that the people can be charged with rioting, and that Paul and the disciples had *not* blasphemed Artemis. Does this remind you of people today who realize that environmental protection may mean less profit for them, but couch themselves in quasi-religious or quasi-patriotic terms to defend their actions?

Yet we would still do well to listen to the core words from the apostles: Act always out of love; act out of the inner spirit:

Knowledge puffs up, but love builds up.

1 Corinthians 8:1

...for the letter kills, but the Spirit gives life.

2 Corinthians 3:6

[23] *All things are lawful, but not all things are beneficial. All things are lawful, but not all things build up.*

[24] *Do not seek your own advantage, but that of the others.*
1 Corinthians 10:23–24

This last verse speaks strongly to me of the current confusion over rights versus responsibilities. In America today freedom is seen almost entirely as the right to make as much money as possible with as little thought as possible to the consequences for others, most especially with as little thought—probably no thought at all—to the future. So we have Hollywood spewing out violence and lurid sex; we have the arms industry playing on the fears of loss of constitutional rights, so the industry can go on raking in money in armaments and ammunition; we have the tobacco companies selling death and lying about it—you know the list. Somewhere along the way, there are real people working for those companies, real people who have abstracted their "legal" actions to such an extent that they've managed to insulate their hearts from taking a deep look at their personal responsibility toward the culture at large.

But let's not feel smug here: The abstractions work for each of us, as we distance our hearts from the effects of our cars' exhaust, the ultimate destination of the garbage we produce, the sewage we flush down the toilets, the lights we forget to turn off, the raw materials we consume, the fact that *we* may view violent or lurid movies or TV programming. We seem to forget that each of us is a member of our own community, and that our "community" stretches from our local towns to the universe.

We need to accept that each of us is responsible for caring for the Earth and one another, and that we must connect our feelings of concern—our love—with action. All the hand-wringing and worrying in the world won't help if we do not put those feelings into action. It *is* tempting to be fatalistic, to despair, but this is the easy way out, the way that leads us to say that we as individuals can do nothing. To do nothing is to deny the responsibility that each of us has in a free society, for that is the true meaning of freedom, I believe: the privilege of acting responsibly.

In the Old Testament, Micah tells us clearly what responsible action is:

> [8] *He has told you, O mortal, what is good, and what does the Lord require of you, but to do justice, and to love kindness, and to walk humbly with your God?*
>
> Micah 6:8

And Christ could not have been more explicit:

> [37] *...Thou shalt love the Lord thy God with all thy heart, and with all thy soul, and with all thy mind.*
> [38] *This is the first and great commandment.*
> [39] *And the second is like unto it: Thou shalt love thy neighbor as thyself.*
> [40] *On these two commandments hang all the law and the prophets.*

Aldo Leopold put it into fresh words in this century:

> *A thing is right when it tends to preserve the integrity, stability, and beauty of the biotic community. It is wrong when it tends otherwise.*
>
> A Sand County Almanac, 1949

Friends have a great head start in responsible action, and we have much guidance from the past. In fact, what has been written about throughout this book *is* Quaker process:

Celebration: remembering to go forth in joy and gratitude, to "walk cheerfully over the earth."

Humility: realizing the depths of our ignorance, and keeping ourselves open to the Light of continuing revelation.

Connectedness: knowing that we are part of Creation—that there is that of the Creator in everything—and that we can have a creative place in it.

Right relationship: questioning whether our words and deeds emerge from a place of harmony and beauty, the place from which the Inner Light comes.

Love: opening ourselves to the "amazing grace" of the Light Within, and radiating out that direct experience of the Inner Light.

Friends' practices of seeking the "sense of the Meeting," combined with the Society's ability to work toward pragmatic solutions, give us great tools in helping bridge some of the deep divisions in society at large. But what about each of us as individuals? What can we do, and how do we go about it? Life has become ever more complicated since John Woolman's day. We scratch our heads over the conundrums: if we buy everything locally, as many thoughtful people suggest, does that mean that people in Third World countries, who already earn little enough from their factory jobs making consumer goods for Americans, will be out of work and won't eat at all?... Should we live in the city, where we can walk or use public transportation—and take up less space with our homes—or should we live in the country where we can grow our own food, but may have to drive to reach jobs, Meeting, and stores, and may contribute to the increasing fragmentation of the land?... Our Meetings are good places to begin to discuss these things, and to help us discern right relationships with one another, money, what we eat and wear, where we live, and how our lives affect the wider earth community [see the section "Using *Caring For Creation: Reflections on the Bibilical Basis of Earthcare* In Your Meeting" for activities you might do in your Meeting to explore these issues, and resources for both individuals and Meetings].

In all of this, we need to make sure that we act out of love, not fanaticism. I remember a Friends' retreat one autumn, where someone decided that we didn't need the lights during worship and turned them off. A Friend rushed from the room in tears; it turned out she was deaf, and without the lights she couldn't read people's lips. That is a very simple example, but it has stuck in my mind as a symbol of how easily over-zealousness can be hurtful and counter-productive.

> *Love does no wrong to a neighbor; therefore, love is the fulfilling of the law.*
> Romans 13:10

In the words of George Fox, how do we go about living "in the virtue of that life and power that [takes] away the occasion of all wars" —war against our fellow human being, war against the rest of Creation? For peace-making and living a life in harmony with Creation are not just about refusing to bear arms, chaining oneself to trees, or marching in protests. They are centered in the day-to-day effort to make our actions correspond with our beliefs, in the seemingly smallest parts of our lives.

But the smallest parts of our lives get little press coverage, much less a salary and benefits. We live in a society that worships the blatant, the hasty, the clever, the glamorous and the glib. And we are seeing what happens to such a society, where movie stars and athletes earn millions while children go hungry; where taxpayers are willing to spend millions on a football stadium but refuse to fund environmental protection; when the majority of adults work outside the home—either from sheer economic necessity or from the desire to own more things—and we no longer take personal care of our children, our elderly, our neighbors. When we do not adequately care for our human community, how can we ever expect our human community to have the energy and resources to care for our other neighbors in Creation?

If I were to live my adult life over again (and assuming I had the luxury of such an economic choice), I would work outside of the home even less than I have, and work harder on the unseen work that binds communities together, the unseen work that is increasingly going undone. "Women's work" has been the glue that helps hold society together. It can be—and should be—done by both men and women. When it is done by neither, society begins to unravel.

In thinking about our modern lives in all their complexity, I see great possibilities for community-building among Friends. Are we aware, in our Meetings, of parents who may be struggling with the modern dilemma of two full-time jobs while raising children? How much do we leave the parents in our Meetings—especially our single parents—to struggle alone? In these days of over-full schedules, how well do we care for our elderly and ill Friends? In our politeness not to invade people's privacy, are we missing chances to knit our community together in love? By helping one another, we help each other to release creative energy that can be used outside our families and Meetings, creativity that is desperately needed in these challenging times.

It is this I see as the major task before me now: to nurture myself, so I can nurture my family, so we can nurture our community, so our community can nurture Creation. To save the whale, we must save the whaler.

Christ tells us: *"Ask, and it will be given you; search, and you will find; knock, and the door will be opened for you"* [Luke 11:9]. I think it's time we started asking, harder than ever—in worship and elsewhere—for guidance in these areas. And we must remember to imagine, to picture the world as it might be.

Can we imagine living differently? Can we imagine living at a healthy pace, a pace that gives room for leisure each day, time for quietness, time for truly being with one another, and for living in the joy of Creation's beauty? Can we imagine economies of caring, where all people are adequately fed and sheltered, where no one is bankrupted by the costs of health care, and where caring for families is truly honored? Can we imagine a world where people are not judged by their gender, skin color, religion, sexual preference, or ethnicity, but instead by the quality of their inner being, and by how that quality is reflected in their lives? Can we imagine a world where the air is clean and the water is pure, where laughter and music are heard more than gunfire, where we are freed from the guilty burden that we are destroying

Creation, where human beings live in the recognition of the sanctity of all life?

That imagining is crucial, along with the belief that each of us has a part to play in healing ourselves and our communities. Laurens Van Der Post reflects:

> *For that was how all real change began; a change of position in some lone, inexperienced and suffering heart... not in great collective resolutions and movements and consensus of established opinion. Only one heart had to find its own true position and travel on from there and all the rest would follow, for no matter how isolated the one felt itself to be, in the deeps of life all were united and no one could move accurately without all ultimately moving with it; just as no star could make a lawful change of course without all the others keeping station with it.*
>
> A Far-Off Place, 1974

From everyone to whom much has been given, much will be required; and from the one to whom much has been entrusted, even more will be demanded.
                                                                Luke 12:48

Using *Caring for Creation: Reflections on the Biblical Basis of Earthcare* in your Meeting

These lessons can be used as a springboard for worship, worship-sharing, discussion, and action in your Meeting. The talks were originally given out of the silence of worship, and when the speaker finished, worship continued.

If there is time, you might listen to an audio tape of one of the talks in each session you hold. Go into worship, take a brief break, and then have worship-sharing or a discussion. (Audiotapes are available; see *Resources* section in this chapter.)

For shorter time frames (such as a 45-minute or hour-long adult First Day School class), participants might be asked to read a chapter before coming to the class, and be prepared to center for worship-sharing or discussion.

Possible activities in studying each chapter

- *Center with worship and/or worship-sharing.*
- *Have people share a verse from the Bible and/or other sources that has inspired them in this direction.*
- *Have queries for discussion or develop queries with the group. (Becoming a Friend to the Creation is a good source of queries and statements from Friends; see Resources section.)*
- *Discuss aspects of Quaker faith and practice that relate to the themes of each chapter.*
- *Have the group discuss how to affect change in their own lives, to come back into right relationship (or how they have been successful in righting themselves in specific areas). Include in the discussion what the challenges and difficulties are in changing, and what specific steps they might take to make the necessary changes.*

Excellent resources to help move forward into action are Jack Phillips's "Walking Gently on the Earth, an Earthcare Checklist" *and* "Earthcare and Soul Care," *and Mary Coelho's* "Let's Get Organized to Care for the Earth: How to Develop a Vital Unity With Nature Group"; *they are listed in* the Resources *section.*

Consider the possibility of discussing each chapter in two or three sessions if one seems too long. The facilitator can choose the appropriate breaks.

Major themes in each chapter

1. Celebration

Bible verses referenced in this chapter:
  Psalms 24:1; 42:1,7; 65:9, 12–13; 66:1; 87:7; 100:1–5; 148:1–13; and 150:6
  Genesis 1:31
  Matthew 8:23
  Amos 5:24
  John 7:37–39
  Isaiah 11:6–9; 55:12–13; and 56:1–2
  Song of Solomon 2:8–14
  John 15:12
  Ecclesiastes 3:1–8 and 8:15
  Exodus 20:8–11

Themes:
- Praising the Creator for the wonder and beauty of Creation: pp. 8–14
- Recognizing the marvels of Creation that are all around us, including our bodies: pp. 14–15
- Cherishing human relationships and the joy of love: p. 15
- Learning to accept the whole pattern of life: p. 16
- Coming into right relationship with time, and "keeping the Sabbath": pp. 16–19
- Celebrating the gift of life and Creation: p. 20

2. Humus

Bible verses referenced in this chapter:
  Job 5:6–7; 12: 7–8; 28:12–28; and 38:4–27
  Isaiah 29:16
  Genesis 8:21
  Exodus 20:23–25

1 Kings 4:29–34
Proverbs 6:6–8 and 30:24–28
Matthew 10:16
1 Corinthians 13

Themes:
- Living in the awareness that we are part of Creation: p. 24
- Recognizing our ignorance of how Creation works and becoming humble: pp. 25–26
- Dealing with the image of human beings as polluters and destroyers, and our cultural tradition of considering human beings as "separate" from Creation: p. 29
- Learning from the wisdom of Creation: pp. 29–34
- Seeking to join humility, knowledge, understanding, and love into wise action: p. 34

3. Connections

Bible verses referenced:
  Matthew 7:12; 22:36–40; and 23:23–24
  Exodus 20:12–17
  Psalm 41:1–2
  Jeremiah 22:13
  Romans 12:4–21
  Matthew 2:18
  Genesis 6:13 and 9:11–13

Themes:
- Understanding who our neighbors are: pp. 38–40
- Recognizing the lack of boundaries between ourselves and other beings: pp. 40–42
- Using imagination to help us understand our interconnectedness and interdependence: pp. 42–48

- Mourning the senseless destruction of Creation, and the human role in that destruction: pp. 48–50
- Seeking God's guidance in learning to "speak to that of God in all Creation": p. 50

4. Right Relationship

Bible verses referenced:
  Matthew 6:19–34
  Leviticus 25:3–4; 25:23–34; and 26:19–20
  Proverbs 2:20–22
  Isaiah 24:4–13 and 32:17
  Hosea 8:7
  1 Timothy 6:9–10
  Mark 10:25
  Psalm 135:15–18
  Ecclesiastes 1:2–11 and 5:10
  Haggai 1:6
  Luke 10:38–42

Themes:
- Learning about human impact on ecosystems: pp. 53–55
- Exploring the Old Testament laws on caring for the land, and why these have not been emphasized historically: pp. 56–58
- Coming to right relationship with wealth and land ownership: pp. 59–61
- Understanding the spiritual effects of wrong relationship with other people and the rest of Creation: p. 61
- Looking at the example of others—such as the life of John Woolman—to help us: pp. 61–66
- Learning to live lives of beauty and integrity, in right relationship: p. 67

5. Stewardship

Bible verses referenced:
- Micah 6:8
- Genesis 1:28
- Romans 13:9–10
- Acts 19:25–27, 34
- 1 Corinthians 8:1 and 10:23–24
- 2 Corinthians 3:6

Themes:
- Understanding the cultural roots of the misuse of God's Creation: pp. 69-70
- Exploring the emphasis on individual ownership and salvation, versus caring for community and being stewards of God's Creation: pp. 70-72
- Discerning what is truly valuable in our lives: p. 72
- Developing new models for living with integrity: pp. 74–75
- Taking responsibility for our actions and their effects on other people and Creation: pp. 76–81
- Exploring how Quaker faith and practices can move us forward: pp. 81–85

Resources

These are a very few of the resources available; many other books, tapes, videos, magazines and pamphlets are available at libraries, bookstores, and via the World Wide Web.

Resources from Friends

Audiotapes of *Caring for Creation: the Biblical Basis of Earthcare*. Lisa L. Gould's Bible Half-hour talks. Available from FCUN.

Becoming a Friend to the Creation: Earthcare Leaven for Friends and Friends Meetings, by Lisa L. Gould. A resource book full of minutes, queries, and statements from Friends Meetings, as well as resources and activities related to spiritually-centered earthcare, 1994. Friends Committee on Unity With Nature (FCUN), 130 pp.

Earthcare and Soul Care, by Jack Phillips. A trifold suggesting how to use the "12-step" method to help one another live more Earth-friendly lives, 1998. Friends Committee on Unity With Nature.

Healing Ourselves and the Earth, by Elizabeth Watson. Friends Committee on Unity With Nature, 1991, reissued 1995, 18 pp.

Let's Get Organized to Care for the Earth: How to Develop a Vital Unity With Nature Group, by Mary Coelho. A trifold describing how to get an earthcare group started. Basic themes include "Changing the Human Heart and Consciousness," "Becoming Informed about the Environmental Situation," "Personal Leadings and Individual and Family Changes," and "Group Projects and Events," 1998. Friends Committee on Unity With Nature.

Walking Gently on the Earth: An Earthcare Checklist, by Jack Phillips. Contains easy-to-follow queries about lifestyles and consumption patterns for individuals and groups who are becoming more sensitive to how their daily lives affect the Earth, 1992. Friends Committee on Unity With Nature.

Resources from beyond Quaker circles

Befriending the Earth: A Theology of Reconciliation Between Humans and the Earth, by Thomas Berry, in dialogue with Thomas Clarke. A discussion of the role of religion in the ecological movement, and how church leaders and individual Christians can help heal the Earth, 1992. Twenty-Third Publications, 157 pp.

Creation Spirituality: Liberating Gifts for the Peoples of the Earth, by Matthew Fox. Learning to use the gift of awe to transform our lives and our relationship with other people and the Earth, 1991. HarperSanFrancisco, 153 pp.

EarthKeeping in the '90s: Stewardship of Creation, edited by Loren Wilkinson. A biblically-based call for responsible stewardship of creation. Revised edition, 1991. Wm. B. Eerdmans Publishing Co., 391 pp.

Living More With Less, by Doris Janzen Longacre. Practical suggestions from the Mennonite Central Committee, to bring a Christian perspective to material consumption, 1980. Herald Press, 294 pp.

Spirit and Nature: Why the Environment is a Religious Issue, edited by Steven C. Rockefeller and John C. Elder. Essays from the world's great religious traditions, on developing Earth awareness, 1992. Beacon Press, 226 pp.

With Roots and Wings: Christianity in an Age of Ecology and Dialogue, by Jay B. McDaniels. Insights from the natural sciences, Christian theology, and interreligious dialogue. 1995. Orbis Books. 243 pp.

Newsletters & magazines:

BeFriending Creation, the bimonthly newsletter of the Friends Committee on Unity With Nature (FCUN), 173-B N. Prospect St., Burlington VT 05401-1607; 802/658-0303. E-mail: fcun@together.net

Creation Care [formerly *Green Cross* magazine], a Christian Environmental Quarterly published by the Evangelical Environmental Network. Available from: EEN, 10 E. Lancaster Ave., Wynnewood, PA 19096-3495; 800/650-6600.

EarthLight, a magazine of spirituality and ecology published by the Friends in Unity With Nature Committee of Pacific Yearly Meeting. Available from FCUN.

Earthkeeping News, the newsletter of the North American Conference on Christianity and Ecology, P.O. Box 40011, Saint Paul, MN 55104; (612) 698-0349. E-mail: 75202.1215@compuserve.com; website: http://www.media.sbexpos.com/nacce.

FCUN has many other trifolds, pamphlets, and books. Contact FCUN for a full listing: FCUN, 173-B N. Prospect St., Burlington VT 05401-1607; 802/ 658-0303. E-mail: fcun@together.net

Literature Cited

Berry, Wendell. 1987. *Home Economics*. San Francisco: North Point Press.

Berry, Wendell. 1986. *The Wild Birds*. San Francisco: North Point Press.

Berry, Wendell. 1993. *Sex, Economy, Freedom, and Community*. New York: Pantheon Books.

Campbell, Joseph. 1988. *The Power of Myth*. New York: Doubleday.

Dawood, N. J. (trans.). 1956. *The Koran*. New York: Penguin Books.

Eiseley, Loren. 1957. *The Immense Journey*. New York: Random House.

Leopold, Aldo. 1949. *A Sand County Almanac*. New York: Oxford University Press.

Metzger, Bruce M. and Roland E. Murphy. 1991. *The New Oxford Annotated Bible, New Revised Standard Version*. New York: Oxford University Press.

Nichols, John T. 1992. What Is a Naturalist, Anyway? *Natural History 101* (11), November 1992.

Nickalls, John L. (Ed.). 1975. *The Journal of George Fox, Rev. Ed*. London: Religious Society of Friends.

Penn, William. 1692. *Some Fruits of Solitude*.

Piercy, Marge. 1982. *Braided Lives*. New York: Summit Books.

Van der Post, Laurens. 1974. *A Far-Off Place*. New York: William Morrow & Co.

Williams, William Carlos. 1954. from "The Host," in *Collected Poems, 1939–1962*. New Directions Publishing Company.

Wilson, E. O. 1992. *The Diversity of Life*. Cambridge: Harvard University Press.

Woolman, John. 1961. *The Journal of John Woolman*, Whittier edition. Secaucus, N.J.: The Citadel Press.

On pp. 53–55:

1. Brown, L. R., C. Flavin, and H. Kane. 1996. *Vital Signs 1996: The Trends That Are Shaping Our Future.* New York: W. W. Norton & Co. 166 pp. (p. 123)
2. Brown, L. 1996. *State of the World 1996: A Worldwatch Institute Report on Progress toward a Sustainable Society.* New York: W. W. Norton & Co. 249 pp. (p. 8)
3. Brown, L. R., C. Flavin, and H. Kane. 1996. *Vital Signs 1996: The Trends That Are Shaping Our Future.* New York: W. W. Norton & Co. 166 pp. (p. 16)
4. *Providence Journal-Bulletin*, "Asthma cases on the upswing," 6 January 1996, p. A4
5. Brown, L. 1996. *State of the World 1996: A Worldwatch Institute Report on Progress toward a Sustainable Society.* New York: W. W. Norton & Co. 249 pp. (p. 126)
6. Brown, L. R., C. Flavin, and H. Kane. 1996. *Vital Signs 1996: The Trends That Are Shaping Our Future.* New York: W. W. Norton & Co. 166 pp. (p. 88)

Permissions and Credits

Excerpts from *A Sand County Almanac* by Aldo Leopold, used with permissionof Oxford University Press.

Excerpt from *The Immense Journey* by Loren Eisley, 1957, Random House, New York, N.Y.

Excerpt from *Braided Lives* by Marge Piercy. Copyright 1982 by Marge Piercy and Middlemarsh, Inc. Published by Summit Books (Simon & Schuster). Used by permission of the Wallace Literary Agency, Inc.

Excerpt from *The Diversity of Life* by E. O. Wilson. Copyright 1992 by Edward O. Wilson. Reprinted by permission of Harvard University Press.

Excerpt from *Home Economics,* by Wendell Berry, 1987, and from *The Wild Birds,* by Wendell Berry, 1986, Farrar, Straus & Giroux (North Point Press), New York, N.Y.

Excerpt from *Sex, Economy, Freedom, and Community,* by Wendell Berry, 1993, Pantheon Books, New York, N.Y.

"You see, I am alive..." an excerpt from *The World of the American Indian,* 1974/1993, National Geographic Society, Washington, D.C. used with permission of the National Geographic Society.

Excerpt from *A Far-Off Place,* by Laurens van der Post, 1974, William Morrow & Co., New York, N.Y.

William Carlos Williams. *Collected Poems,* 1939–1962. Copyright 1954 by William Carlos Williams. Used with permission of New Directions Publishing Corporation. Selection from "The Host."